Puppies Are Special Friends

By Joanne Ryder
Illustrated by James Spence

*The author wishes to thank Charles McGinley and Cheryl Maller of the
North Shore Animal League for their kind help in researching this book.*

MERRIGOLD PRESS • NEW YORK

When puppies are born, they cannot see or hear. At first, puppies can only crawl. They spend their days close to their mother, drinking her milk and sleeping.

Collies

After a few weeks, puppies grow curious. They sniff at their mother. They sniff at the other puppies nearby. The world around them is full of interesting smells.

Their eyes open up, and they slowly begin to see things—their big warm mother, their sisters and brothers.

Then puppies begin to hear sounds. Too much noise frightens them. A loud crash startles them. Soft voices soothe them.

As puppies grow stronger they become tiny explorers. They can walk and run. They sniff and lick and chew new things. Puppies begin to learn more and more about their world.

They also learn about each other. Puppies need to play with other puppies. By playing and pretend-fighting, puppies learn how to get along with each other. If they do not learn this when they are young, they will always be shy with other dogs when they grow up.

German Shepherd

As puppies grow bigger they need to play with people, too. Puppies should be touched gently and held carefully. That way they learn that people will treat them kindly and protect them. The friendliest dogs learned to be comfortable with people when they were puppies.

Cocker Spaniel

When a puppy's owner plays with it and takes care of it, the puppy thinks that person is a dog, too! The owner becomes part of a puppy's family or pack and can begin to teach the puppy to obey him or her as it would obey its parents.

Puppies and people can learn to be friends.
Puppies try to understand what people want them
to do. But puppies do not understand words. They
learn to recognize different tones of voice.

When a puppy hears someone speak to it in a
gruff tone of voice, it knows it is being scolded.

Basset Hound

But when someone calls the puppy with a light, happy tone, the puppy runs eagerly toward him. Perhaps it is time to play!

Labrador Retriever

Black Labrador Retriever

A puppy's strongest sense is its sense of smell.
It sniffs at new things because it learns about
them from their scent.

A dog can learn to find an object by its scent.
The thing may look like other objects nearby. But
if it was touched by someone the dog knows, the
dog can smell the person's scent on it.

Dogs have a much better sense of smell than people do. When a puppy smells someone, it can often tell how that person is feeling. When a person is angry or sick, her body has a different scent than when she is calm or feeling healthy.

Sometimes even the most lively dog will stay quietly near someone who is sick. It can smell that the person is not feeling well.

Fox Terrier

People touch things with their fingers. Puppies touch things with their mouths. A puppy may tug at someone's hand or clothing to get him to play.

Boxer

Puppies' mouths are sensitive. When puppies are born, they have no teeth. Soon tiny milk teeth grow. In a few months these teeth are replaced by larger permanent teeth.

Because they are playful and curious, puppies like to chew things. They learn about things by "mouthing" them. Chewing also helps a puppy's new teeth break through. A rawhide or nylon bone is a good chewing toy for a puppy.

Saint Bernard

Shetland Sheepdog

Miniature Dachshund

West Highland White Terrier

Labrador Retriever

There are many different kinds, or breeds, of dogs. But all puppies look a bit alike. They are small and cute. They have round bodies and round heads with big eyes. Their fur is short and silky.

But puppies change as they grow. When they grow up, they will look more like their parents.

A West Highland white terrier is a lively dog with a good sense of hearing. When it hears an intruder, it barks a warning.

A Labrador retriever is a popular pet.

Look how different these full-grown dogs are. Some are still fairly small, but others are very large.

Some breeds of dogs are known for having special traits. Some are calmer than others. Some are easier to train. Some are better watchdogs or guard dogs.

A Shetland sheepdog has long fur and needs to be groomed often.

A Saint Bernard can weigh over 150 pounds.

An adult miniature dachshund can weigh less than 10 pounds.

If you get a puppy for a pet, you need to help it stay healthy. Puppies should be checked by a veterinarian, or animal doctor, when they are young. They need shots to protect them against dog diseases.

Puppies need fresh food and water to stay healthy. They need a bed in a warm, quiet place. They need regular grooming and a safe teething toy to chew.

Puppies are alert, loving pets. They can learn to obey household rules. Training a puppy to obey requires patience and kindness. Puppies need clear, simple commands so they can learn to understand. You need to repeat the command in the same way every time.

Poodle

Puppies are baby dogs, and like all babies, they make mistakes. You need to say no to a puppy when it does something wrong. But you should never yell at a puppy or hit it.

Kind, consistent training helps a puppy learn how to be part of your world.

Dutch Decoy Dog

A puppy is a special pet. You can watch it grow and help it learn. You can play together and grow up together. You can learn about each other in many ways.

And, most of all, you can be each other's very special friend.